NATC

CRAYOLA CHRISTMAS COLORS

MARI SCHUH

LERNER PUBLICATIONS ◆ MINNEAPOLIS

FOR FAIRMONT, MY FESTIVE HOMETOWN

Official Licensed Product
Lerner Publications Company
A division of Lerner Publishing Group, Inc.
241 First Avenue North
Minneapolis, MN 55401 USA

For reading levels and more information, look up this title at www.lernerbooks.com.

Main body text set in Billy Infant Regular 24/30.
Typeface provided by SparkyType.

Library of Congress Cataloging-in-Publication Data

The Cataloging-in-Publication Data for Crayola Christmas Colors is on file at the Library of Congress.
ISBN 978-1-5415-1089-0 (lib. bdg.)
ISBN 978-1-5415-2745-4 (pbk.)
ISBN 978-1-5415-1242-9 (eb pdf)

Manufactured in the United States of America
1-43973-33987-1/19/2018

TABLE OF CONTENTS

A COLORFUL CHRISTMAS

It's Christmastime!

Christmas is full of bright colors. **RED** and **GREEN** are all around!

Colors bring holiday cheer during Christmas.

Bright lights twinkle at night.

How many colors do you see?

Christmas Day is on December 25.

GETTING READY

Colorful ornaments sparkle on **GREEN**
Christmas trees.
Christmas lights decorate homes.

Children wear cozy **RED** Santa hats.

Some write letters to Santa.

Many people send Christmas cards to family and friends.

RED-and-**GREEN** stockings hang above the warm fireplace.

Soon they will be full of gifts!

Children tell Santa their
Christmas wishes.

His big beard is fluffy
and **WHITE**.

What do you wish for?

CHRISTMAS FUN

Yummy Christmas cookies are fun to make.

Frosting and sprinkles make snowmen, reindeer, and much more!

RED-and-**WHITE** candy canes are sweet Christmas treats. Gingerbread houses are fun to make and eat!

What's your favorite Christmas treat?

It's fun to get gifts at Christmas. It's also fun to give them to others!

COLORFUL gifts are piled under the Christmas tree.

What could be inside?

CHRISTMAS AROUND THE WORLD

People celebrate Christmas all around the world.

Christmas in Mexico is full of color and fun.

Children break the piñatas. Then candy and toys fall out!

BLUE, RED, and GREEN paper covers bright piñatas.

BLUE skies and **TAN** sandy beaches are a part of Christmas too.

Some people in Australia celebrate Christmas on the beach!

MERRY AND BRIGHT

Colors make Christmas merry and bright.

Merry Christmas to all!

COPY AND COLOR!

Here are some of the Crayola® crayon colors used in this book. Can you find all of these colors in the photos? Copy these pages, and color the symbols of Christmas.

YELLOW ORANGE

PINE GREEN

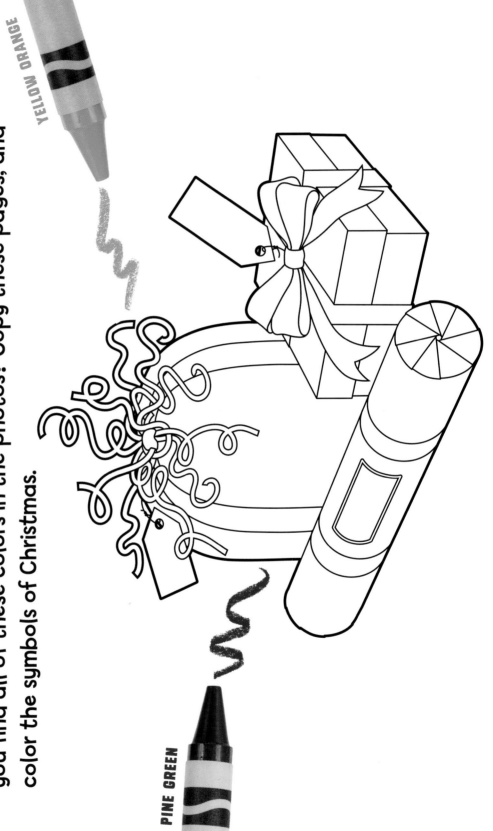

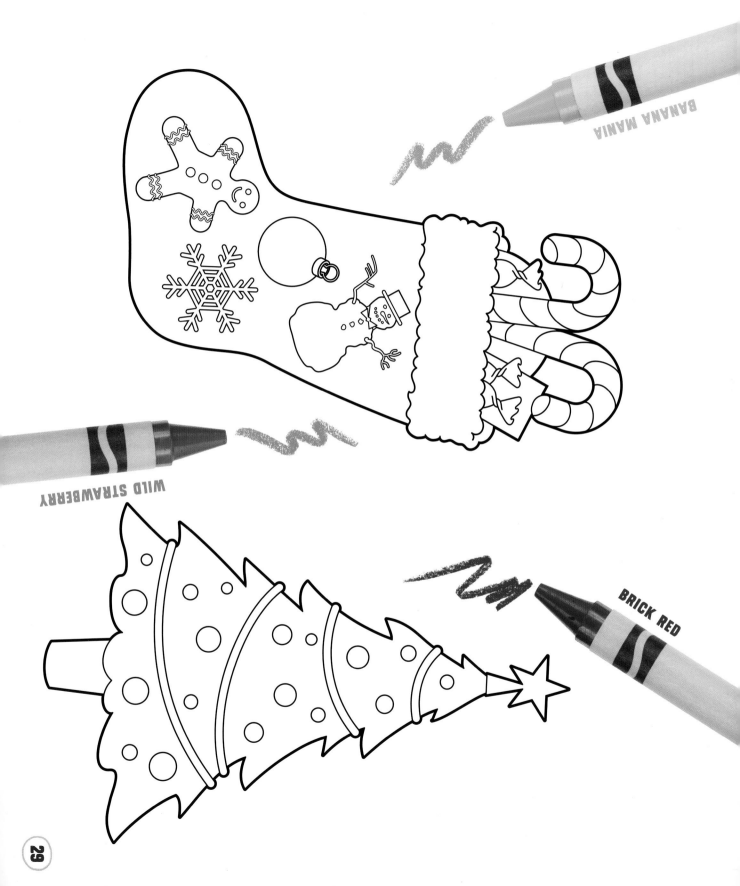

BANANA MANIA

WILD STRAWBERRY

BRICK RED

GLOSSARY

Australia: a continent in the South Pacific Ocean

celebrate: to do something special for an important event or holiday

gingerbread: a cake or cookie that is flavored with ginger and other spices

merry: very happy and cheerful

Mexico: a country that borders the United States

ornaments: small, pretty objects used to decorate Christmas trees

piñatas: decorated containers filled with candy and toys

reindeer: a type of deer with large antlers that lives in far northern areas

TO LEARN MORE

BOOKS

Friedman, Laurie. *Merry Christmas, Mary Christmas!* Minneapolis: Carolrhoda Books, 2017.
The Christmas family loves Christmas. They have the biggest tree and the most lights.
But seven-year-old Mary has a plan to make this year's celebration the best yet.

Lindeen, Mary. *Christmas.* Chicago: Norwood House, 2016.
Read about the traditions and symbols of the Christmas season.

Sebra, Richard. *It's Christmas!* Minneapolis: Lerner Publications, 2017.
Learn the many ways people celebrate Christmas.

WEBSITES

Activity Village: Christmas
https://www.activityvillage.co.uk/christmas
Find fun Christmas activities, crafts, and recipes to try!

Crayola: Christmas Wish Stocking
http://www.crayola.com/crafts/christmas-wish-stocking-craft/
Make a colorful Christmas stocking covered with your holiday wishes.

National Geographic Kids: Winter Celebrations
http://kids.nationalgeographic.com/explore/winter-celebrations/
Discover how people celebrate winter holidays, including Christmas.

INDEX

PHOTO ACKNOWLEDGMENTS

The images in this book are used with the permission of: Brent Hofacker/Shutterstock.com, pp. 1, 18; chasiki/Shutterstock.com, pp. 2, 30, 31, 32; nicolesy/iStock/Getty Images, p. 4; Africa Studio/Shutterstock.com, p. 5 (top left); Aneese/iStock/Getty Images, p. 5 (top right); AnnaElizabeth photography/Shutterstock.com, p. 5 (bottom left); stockphoto-graf/Shutterstock.com, p. 5 (bottom right); fotocraft/Shutterstock.com, pp. 6–7; kali9/E+/Getty Images, p. 8; JurgaR/iStock/Getty Images, p. 11; Alexander Raths/Shutterstock.com, pp. 14–15; acongar/Shutterstock.com, p. 16; SelectStock/Vetta/Getty Images, p. 19; elenaleonova/E+/Getty Images, p. 20; DGLimages/iStock/Getty Images, p. 21; © Todd Strand/Independent Picture Service, p. 22; erlucho/Shutterstock.com, p. 23; Scott Barbour/Getty Images, p. 24; Mirelle/Shutterstock.com, p. 25; Monkey Business Images/Shutterstock.com, p. 27; © Laura Westlund/Independent Picture Service, pp. 28, 29.

Cover: acongar/Shutterstock.com (cookies); Brent Hofacker/Shutterstock.com (candy); small1/Shutterstock.com (ornaments); LeoWolfert/Shutterstock.com (gifts).